DON'T QUIT

Inspirational Poetry

DON'T QUIT

*Inspirational Poetry
by
Mychal Wynn*

RISING SUN PUBLISHING
1012 Fair Oaks Boulevard
South Pasadena, CA 91030
(800) 524-2813

FIRST PRINTING, 1990
SECOND PRINTING, 1992

ISBN 1–880463–25–3, cloth
ISBN 1–880463–26–1, paper

DON'T QUIT – Inspirational Poetry
Copyright © 1990 Mychal Wynn

Rising Sun Publishing
1012 Fair Oaks Boulevard
South Pasadena, California 91030
(800) 524-2813

Printed in the United States of America.

Dedication

This book is dedicated to my first born, Mychal-David Isiah.

I give to him my thoughts, my strength, and my belief in a brighter tomorrow.

May this encourage him to expand his own thoughts, gain his own strength, and contribute to the brilliance of today.

Acknowledgments

I thank my wife for her love, support, and undying encouragement as I have made the journey from engineer, to entrepreneur, to poet, to author, to publisher, to husband, and father. Our family has been blessed in ways more abundant than we could have ever imagined.

We have been blessed through the leadership and spiritual empowerment of Dr. Frederick K.C. Price, III and the ministry of Crenshaw Christian Center in Los Angeles, California.

I thank my editor, Anita Luckie, for her critical review and positive encouragement. And, I thank God, who divinely guides us to share His inspiration and what we believe are powerful affirmations.

Contents

How to use this book

This book should be used in the classroom through oral recitation. To submit such positive ideals to memory is to integrate them into one's own thoughts. To speak the words, indeed brings these ideals to life. Students should be encouraged to discuss and expand upon such concepts as diligence, determination, courage, internal strength, spiritual strength, and perseverance. This book should be used by entrepreneurs, executives, and managers to encourage their employees. Our work place can be extraordinarily strengthened through the communication and encouragement of the ideals inherent within Mychal's poetry. Each poem lends itself to be posted on a bulletin board offering spiritual uplift for continued commitment to one's personal goals and business objectives.

This book should be shared with our children, relatives, friends, and others for daily encouragement. Few among us would not benefit from an uplifting thought. All can share in the idea that working together for a higher good with the strength and determination to persevere when confronted by obstacles is what leads us forward into a better tomorrow.

We believe that once you pick up this book, you will have difficulty putting it down. Most will simply read it from beginning to end in the first reading. However, we suggest that you pause after each poem and reflect on how it pertains to your life and your personal philosophy of living. We then suggest that you reread it and think of someone you know who would be encouraged by that particular verse.

We believe that those who enjoy poetry will enjoy this book, and those who have never purchased a book of poetry will find a special place for this book. We gladly anticipate that the poems and quotes contained here will be repeated at graduation ceremonies, in athletic locker rooms, in classrooms, in churches, at banquets, at business meetings and by all who seek to bring hope and encouragement to others.

From the author

The verses in this book represent my personal affirmations. Through verbally affirming these verses I hope that you will, as my pastor would say, "Speak life unto your life." The affirmations contained in this book have been second nature to me. They have represented philosophies of living that have guided my life. The cornerstone of this book, the poem "*Don't Quit*," is actually an adaptation of an anonymous poem by the same title that I was introduced to in the second grade at Edmund Burke Elementary School in Chicago, Illinois. A teacher read the poem to the class, and although I forgot many of the words, the title "Don't Quit," became embedded in my subconscious. So much so, that during high school, I wrote my version of "Don't Quit" which has become the guiding philosophy of my life.

In traveling throughout the country conducting workshops, and presenting keynote addresses at banquets and luncheons, I have been led by the Spirit to speak to others about the power of the spirit dwelling within them. A power unimaginable. A power so great that mountains become mole hills. That obstacles which appear insurmountable are easily overcome. That problems which appear unsolvable are resolved by solutions which become amazingly clear. To those who understand the power and authority promised by God, and received through Christ, you will feel the spirit in this book. To those who have not yet received, I hope that you will read and enjoy the affirmations contained in this book. Perhaps one of the verses will touch you as I was touched in the second grade. Perhaps you will discover a verse that will become your philosophy of living and empower you to cope with, and successfully overcome, any challenges confronting you in your life.

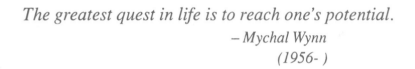

The greatest quest in life is to reach one's potential.
– Mychal Wynn
(1956-)

Born to Win

Some are born to become Eagles
    To spread their wings and fly
    With strength and perseverance
    Continue reaching toward the sky

Others will be as Lions
    Standing tall, proud, and free
    Their faith and determination
    Offering a light for all to see

The Rams will stand on mountaintops
    Greeting the dawn of each new day
    Prepared to meet whatever obstacles
    That should dare to block their way

They all stand before the rising Sun
    With a sense of pride that stands the test
    That challenges all who dare to dream
    To dare become the best

That which caused us trial shall yield us triumph; and that which made our heart ache shall fill us with gladness. The only true happiness is to learn, to advance, and to improve; which could not happen unless we had commence with error, ignorance, and imperfection. We must pass through the darkness, to reach the light.

— Albert Pike
(1809-1891)

THERE'S A NEW DAY COMING

When the Sun announces the dawning day
Just flex your muscles and start on your way
Go over, or under, around, or through
Any obstacles or hurdles that challenge you
There's a new day coming

Cast aside the failures of yesterday
Forget the peaks and valleys that have paved your way
Wipe the sweat from your brow and the dust from your shoe
Take a breath and relax so that you may begin anew
There's a new day coming

Forget the burdens and obstacles that have held you back
Focus on your dreams and prepare a plan of attack
There are battles awaiting to challenge your success
Daring you to stand tall and to give it your best
There's a new day coming

No matter how great the journey, or how heavy the load
How steep the mountain, or how rough the road
When your arms grow weary and legs give way
Stop and rest for a moment, it will be okay
There's a new day coming

As shadows spring forth from the setting Sun
Take a moment and savor the battles you've won
Sleep peacefully tonight and enjoy your rest
Awaken tomorrow and continue your quest
There's always, a new day coming

The diamond cannot be polished without friction, nor the man perfected without trials.

— Chinese Proverb

YESTERDAY HAS LEFT YOU FOREVER

YESTERDAY has left you forever

 You cannot relive it
 You cannot undo the things that were done
 You cannot retrieve the words that were spoken
 You cannot pull back the blows that were thrown

TOMORROW is forever out of your reach

 You cannot live it today
 Nor can you substitute it for yesterday
 You cannot live your life waiting for it to come

TODAY is always with you

 You can live it to its fullest
 You can always give it your best
 It is always the first day
  of the rest of your life

The only certainty about following the crowd is that you will all get there together.

— *Mychal Wynn*
(1956-)

BE THE CAPTAIN OF YOUR SHIP

Be the Captain of your ship
and follow your dreams wherever they lead
allow the winds of faith to fill your sail
and be patient as you set your speed

Witness the brilliance of the rising Sun
whose rays reach across your bow
warming your spirit as they guide you forward
reassuring your faith somehow

And during the days when the sky has darkened
transforming a quiet to a stormy sea
remain steadfast and determined
to continue sailing to where you want to be

Although others may turn their ships around
afraid to ever again leave shore
simply drop your anchor until the storm has passed
then hoist your sail once more

There is beauty to be found in all the world
as faith guides your ship to sea
there is joy to be found in companionship
and in solitude you'll find serenity

To be the Captain of your ship
requires you to chart your way
to believe in yourself and in your dreams
and to maintain your course each day

When you sail your ship toward the horizon
the only guarantee of what you'll find
is that you'll never hunger for what might have been
through your courage you'll gain peace of mind

Reputation is what men and women think of us;
Character is what God and angels know of us.
                                    – Paine
                                (1737-1809)

DARE

DARE to be different
> when all around you seek conformity

DARE to encounter obstacles
> when all around you avoid conflict

DARE to seek possibilities
> when all around you see only the impossible

DARE to seek new and greater challenges
> when all around you are procrastinating

DARE to remain strong
> when all around you are weakening

DARE to continue
> when all around you are quitting

DARE to have faith
> when all around you are doubting

DARE to dream
> even if no one dreams with you

One should act in consonance with the way of heaven and earth, which is enduring and eternal. The superior man perseveres long in his course, adapts to the times, but remains firm is his direction and correct in his goals.

— *I Ching*
(B.C. 1150)

Be a Winner

If all around you are quitting, as they sometimes do
If your critics are many and friends are few
If obstacles confront you at every turn
Remember the lessons that Winners learned . . .

To stop and quit you will never win
Until you decide to try it again
When life's little hurdles slow you down
Just steady your pace and hold your ground

Hold fast to your dreams, as they can come true
When you do the best that you can possibly do
To win you must believe that you will not fail
Perseverance is the breeze that fills your sail

Although the unexpected may rock your boat
Winners will weather the storm remaining afloat
Conceive it, believe it, and know that you can
Continue step by step according to plan

Stand up and be counted so that the world will see
That you believe in becoming the best you can be
Accept the challenges of life and you'll continue to find
That winning is the spirit of living
        . . . it's merely a state of mind

I love those who can smile in trouble, who can gather strength from distress, and grow brave by reflection. 'Tis the business of little minds to shrink, but they whose heart is firm, and whose conscience approves their conduct, will pursue their principles unto death.

— *Paine*

(1737-1809)

LIFE IS OFTEN DIFFICULT

When life is most difficult
>   we must hold fast to our dreams

When the answers are unclear
>   we must maintain our faith

When the obstacles are greatest
>   we must continue our pace

The impossible can only exist
When we no longer believe
>   in the existence of possibilities

Success is to be measured not so much by the position that one has reached in life as by the obstacles which one has overcome while trying to succeed.

– Booker T. Washington
(1856-1915)

SUCCESS

Success is awarded those
   who dream of endless possibilities
   who, through determination
      and perseverance,
   continue climbing mountains
   and following rainbows

The struggles which we endure
      the battles in which we engage
      the conflicts which we encounter
   help us to gain
      a greater perspective of life
   it is the benefit of these experiences
      that give our lives meaning

A wise man never knows all, only fools know everything.

– African Proverb

If YOU AND I SHOULD DIFFER

If you and I should differ
> in our beliefs
> in our philosophies
> in our understanding of things

We may come to realize
> it is not important
> that we always agree

Only that we respect each other's
> right to be different

Only that we respect each other's
> right to be heard

Prosperity is no just scale; adversity is the only balance to weigh friends.

– Plutarch

(44-120 A.D.)

IF YOU ARE MY FRIEND

IF YOU ARE MY FRIEND
    be honest with me
    even if it hurts

IF YOU ARE MY FRIEND
    push me forward
    when I want to quit

IF YOU ARE MY FRIEND
    acknowledge my faults
    and help me to correct them

IF YOU ARE MY FRIEND
    be critical of me
    when I am not critical of myself

IF YOU ARE MY FRIEND
    I can turn to you
    during difficult times

IF YOU ARE MY FRIEND
    I can cry around you
    and not be ashamed

IF YOU ARE MY FRIEND
    I can share my feelings
    and not offend you

IF YOU ARE MY FRIEND
    all these things I will do for you

A tree is known by its fruit; a man by his deeds. A good deed is never lost; he who sows courtesy reaps friendship, and he who plants kindness gathers love.

– Basil

(329-379 A.D.)

A Pledge Of Friendship

I'll always do the best I can
    to listen, share, and understand
I'll always respect your point of view
As long as you remember
    I have one too!
I'll push when I can,
    and pull when I must
There's no room for jealousy,
    when there's genuine trust
I'll share in your dreams,
    and in the burdens you bear
In your joy, sadness,
    hope, and despair
Although the future is uncertain,
    the present is sure
We may occasionally disagree,
    but true friends endure

We can do anything we want to do if we stick to it long enough.

– Helen Keller
(1880-1968)

A PLEDGE TO MYSELF

Today I pledge to be

the best possible me
No matter how good I am
I know that I can become better

Today I pledge to build

on the work of yesterday
Which will lead me
into the rewards of tomorrow

Today I pledge to feed

my mind: knowledge
my body: strength, and
my spirit: faith

Today I pledge to reach

new goals
new challenges, and
new horizons

Today I pledge to listen

to the beat of my drummer
who leads me onward
in search of dreams

Today I pledge to believe in me

Vision looks inward and becomes duty.
Vision looks outward and becomes aspiration.
Vision looks upward and becomes faith.

— Stephen S. Wise
(1874-1949)

A CREED OF FAITH

Life holds for you no guarantees
    It may be a stairway growing steeper
Yet if you take each step stride after stride
    You'll grow stronger, instead of weaker

You'll have your ups, and you'll have your downs
    And even when you make it through
There may be times you'll feel, you can't go on
    That there's nothing more that you can do

It's during those times of doubting,
    During those moments of great despair
That you must lift your head up to the sky
    Asking for guidance through your prayer

Ask the Lord to give you the strength
    To make it through another day
Stare each of your problems in the face
    Never yielding, and simply say

"I will do the best that I can do
    I won't let anything hold me down
I'll concede the battle, not the war
    I will always come back around

God within me, there is nothing before me
    That can block the way that I must go
The obstacles that lie in my path
    May make the going slow

But I'll never quit, thus, I will not fail
    And in my life you'll always see
That I will give it all that I've got
    I will become the best that I can be!"

The way of a superior man is threefold:
Virtuous, he is free from anxieties;
Wise, he is free from perplexities;
Bold, he is free from fear.

– *Confucius*
(B.C. 551-479)

I AM

I am strong

I am gentle

I am proud

I am humble

I am confident

I am beautiful

I am intelligent

I am becoming all that I can be

I am a child of God

The Eternal looked upon me for a moment with His eye of power, and annihilated me in His being, and became manifest to me in His essence. I saw I existed through Him.

— Jala-Uddin Rumi
(1207-1273)

Thank You Father

Thank you Father,

For the brilliance of your light
guiding my way through all adversity

For the depth of your shadow
reassuring my faith and protecting me from evil

For the strength of your hand
enabling me to stand tall and strong

For the magnificence of your wisdom
always providing the answer to my prayer

For the peace I've found
since knowing you,
    my Heavenly Father

Difficulties show men what they are. In case of any difficulty remember that God has pitted you against a rough antagonist that you may be a conqueror, and this cannot be without toil.

— Epictetus
(50-138 A.D.)

Walking In His Light

When all around you move at a different pace
> or in different directions

When you have set your sights on goals
> beyond the vision of others

When you've tired from your battles
> having grown weary from your struggles

Go and find a quiet place
> to seek council with your Heavenly Father

Trust in Him
> for the answers to your questions
> and the strength to wage your battles

When you seek Him, you'll discover

If you walk in His light
> you will move at the right pace
> and walk in the right direction

Great men are they who see that spiritual is stronger than any material force, that thoughts rule the world.

— *Ralph Waldo Emerson*
(1803-1882)

THE SPIRIT WITHIN YOU

The magnificence of the Universe
    Its beauty and energy
    Its wisdom and understanding
Are one with the spirit
dwelling within you

The stars are beacons
Beckoning you onward
    challenging you to dream
    encouraging you to believe

No journey is so far
    that the Spirit cannot lead you

No burden is so great
    that the Spirit cannot strengthen you

Without the Spirit
    the smallest obstacle appears insurmountable

With the Spirit
    you are powerful and unyielding
    diligent and determined
Capable of becoming
    all that you were created to be

The block of granite which was an obstacle in the path of the weak, becomes a steppingstone in the path of the strong.

– Carlyle
(1797-1881)

OVERCOMING DARKNESS

There is a great wall
    surrounding each of us
invisible, yet firm
each brick solidly joined
blocking the light
    challenging us to dream
to believe in things unseen
to dare reach for things unreachable

The wall is unyielding
splattered with the blood and sweat
    of those who dared
cemented stronger
    by those who quit
It has shattered the dreams
of the most optimistic

Yet the strength of this wall
    is an illusion
destroyed by unwavering faith
each brick giving way
    to a ray of hope
The more you persevere
the more it crumbles before you
Standing on your faith
    enables you
to stand triumphantly in the light
Where you discover
    it is the fear of failure
    that darkens the minds
of those without faith

The ultimate measure of a man is not where he stands in moments of comfort and convenience, but where he stands at times of challenge and controversy.

– Dr. Martin Luther King, Jr.
(1929-1968)

DIGNITY

Dignity is the ability
to stand strong and tall
in the face of adversity
While being able
to bow to the elderly
and crawl with the children

Dignity is taking a stand
for your beliefs
Without closing your mind
to another's opinion

Dignity is being an example
by your deeds
and through your words
avoiding gossip, anger, and lies

Dignity will manifest itself in
the warmth of your smile,
the depth of your love,
and kindness for your fellowman

Trials teach us what we are; they dig up the soil, and let us see what we are made of.

– Charles Spurgeon
(1834-1892)

ATTITUDE OR CHANCE?

There were two seeds
  tilled in the same soil
  sowed with the same plow
Each growing stronger
  filled with dreams
  and aspirations
  pouring sweat into the land
  filling the soil with pain
One becoming firmly rooted
  reaching upward to the light
  strong in purpose
  steadfast in conviction
The other,
  growing weak
  trembling in the wind
The victim of many battles
  humbled and beaten
  withered and worn
How have their lives taken
  such different directions?
Although they were
  tilled in the same soil and
  sowed with the same plow

*He who endeavors to serve, to benefit, and improve
the world, is like a swimmer, who struggles against a
rapid current, in a river lashed into angry waves by
the wind. Often they roar over his head, often they
beat him back and baffle him. Most men yield to the
stress of the current . . . Only here and there the stout,
strong heart and vigorous arms struggle on toward
ultimate success.*

– Albert Pike
(1809-1891)

WHO ARE WE . . .

Who are we . . .
     If we do not raise our voice
          against injustice
     If we do not speak out
          for truth and righteousness?
Who are we . . .
     If we do not extend our hands
          to those in need
     If we do not share our light
          with those in darkness?
Who are we . . .
     To hate those who
          look differently,
          speak differently, or
          believe differently?
Who are we . . .
     If we cannot encourage others
          without envy
     If we cannot share in their success
          without jealousy?
Our garden results
          from the seeds we've sown
Our house stands
          on the foundation we've laid
Our life will be measured
          by the things we've done
Who are we?

He only is exempt from failures who makes no efforts.
– Richard Whately
(1787-1863)

IF WE DO NOT TRY

If we do not enter the race

    we surely cannot lose

If we do not exercise independence

    we may never have to choose

If we do not decide to try

    we certainly cannot fail

If we don't put our ship to sea

    we surely will not sail

If we don't attempt to learn

    no one can criticize our I.Q.

If we refuse to accept life's challenges

    we can't fail at what we do

But to live our lives in darkness

    through the fear of what we'll see

Is to rob the world of a piece of itself

    . . . a piece of beauty that will never be

Faced with crisis, the man of character falls back on himself. He imposes his own stamp of action, takes responsibility for it, makes it his own.

– Charles De Gaulle
(1890-1970)

WINNING ISN'T EVERYTHING

It's often said that, "Winning isn't everything,
   it's the only thing."
Yet the definition of winning
   is a very personal thing.
It isn't always coming in number one.
It's being satisfied
   that you've given your best.
It's that good feeling
   of knowing that you didn't quit.
It's knowing that you're never as good
   as you're going to be.
It's being pleased with your effort,
   and being pleased with yourself.

Think like a man of action, act like a man of thought.
– Henri Louis Bergson
(1859-1941)

A MAN IS . . .

A man is not quick to anger

    he's not one whose quick to brawl
If you see a man bullying others
    he's not a man at all

A man is not a quitter

    he's not one to turn and run
When the going gets rough, he gets tough
    he'll remain 'til the job is done

A man takes no satisfaction

    in seeing another fail
He encourages all to try
    and to believe that they can prevail

A man will never boast or brag

    or kick sand in your eye
He'll stand firm on his conviction
    with his head held to the sky

A man will always lend a hand

    when he finds a friend in need
His character and his integrity
    makes him a true friend indeed

*We are always in the forge, or on the anvil; by trials,
God is shaping us for higher things.*
— Beecher
(1813-1878)

DON'T QUIT

When people pull you down, as they often will
When the battle you're fighting is all uphill
When the funds are low and the debts are high
When you're laughing, although you'd rather cry
When you discover yourself slowing down a bit
Stop and take a deep breath, but don't you quit

Although you've worked so hard just to get this far
You must steady your pace, just to stay where you are
You'll need twice the effort to make your way
Tomorrow won't come, until you've conquered today
And if you discover yourself slowing down a bit
Stop and rest if you must, but don't you quit

Always do the best that you can possibly do
Treasure true friends who are far and few
Never give up, whatever the burden you bear
Just one more step might get you there
Often the battle that is proceeding slow
Will conclude abruptly, when dealt another blow

Succeed in believing that you will not fail
Use diligence and determination to set your sail
When the weather is stormy and the waters are rough
In the moment of peril the strong get tough
Whenever life presses you down a bit
Stand up and shout, "I will not quit!"

Let your light so shine before men,
that they will see your good works,
and glorify your Father which is in heaven.
                                        – Saint Matthew 5:16

THE LEGACY LIVES

My father took his worthy name
    and passed it on to me
He marveled not at what I was
    but at what I was to be
He taught me all that he knew
    and challenged me to learn the rest
He taught me to believe in myself
    and to always give my best
His arms were strong and his smile was soft
    he had his own special way
He never complained about what he hadn't done
    he simply gave his best each day
He sowed a garden whose beauty blooms
    during the most difficult of days
The seeds of diligence, determination,
    optimism, strength, and praise
The legacy of my father lives
    his light shines for all to see
As long as I stand before the world
    becoming the best that I can be

If you wish to know the mind of a man, listen to his words.

– Chinese Proverb